SEA WOLF

BY JACK LONDON

LEVEL D — HIGH INTERMEDIATE — 1250 BASIC WORDS

Adapted by Elaine Kirn

- UCLA American Language Center
- Santa Monica College
- Los Angeles Unified School District

Regents Publishing Company, Inc.
2 Park Avenue, New York, N.Y. 10016

INTRODUCTION

As researchers conclude that reading in a second language is not substantially different from reading in one's native language, it is becoming clear that one task of ESL instruction is to train learners to approach texts in English much as they approach those in their own language. Students need to be weaned from their dictionaries and their arduous translation methods so that they can begin to read with confidence and ease. It is also becoming clear that people learn to read better, in any language, simply by reading. Thus, another task of ESL instruction is to provide learners with materials that motivate further reading.

The *Regents Illustrated Classics* series is designed to motivate low-level reading through highly appealing stories which have all the excitement, action, and universal themes of the well-known classics on which they are based. The stories are presented in a fully illustrated format and are written within strict vocabulary and structure limits so that students can read almost immediately with some of the same confidence they feel when reading in their own language.

The illustrated format is an effective teaching tool in our visually oriented society, where students are used to learning through images and are often intimidated by uninterrupted pages of text. The illustrations immediately connect the printed word to a recognizable context and provide visual clues to vocabulary and plot. The picture panels, with their sophisticated drawings and easy-to-read type, can be used a variety of ways to facilitate the reading process.

The readers are divided into four levels. Levels A and B are for beginning students and levels C and D for intermediate students. Level A is intended for learners who have nearly completed a basic language course and is based on a list of 500 frequently used words. Level B is based on a cumulative list of 750 words. Stories in the beginning levels are told in the present tenses, except when other tenses are needed to preserve the authenticity of the narrative. Levels C and D use all major tenses and structures; the list for level C contains 1000 words while the list for level D contains 1250. Any vocabulary not included on the base list for a particular level is given in the "Vocabulary" section of the reader and is generally defined in the glossary.

Another goal in the series is the active teaching of reading skills. Readers are divided into three parts; each part is introduced by a "Getting Started" section consisting of pictures to stimulate interest in the story and questions to focus attention on the main events. Each part ends with several pages of exercises, entitled "Getting the Main Idea," "Understanding Details," and "Building Vocabulary." A section called "Summarizing" at the end of the readers leads to student discussion of the story. Since exercises concentrate on comprehension and vocabulary-building, the readers are also appropriate for native speakers of English who want to develop basic reading skills.

Suggestions for using the various features of the readers are given in the teacher's manuals. There is one manual for levels A and B and one for levels C and D. The manuals also contain answer keys for all exercises and ideas for additional reading activities.

Thanks to Tim Welch at IPS Publishing: He developed this series. Marjorie Walsleben gave unequaled editorial help. Etc. Graphics labored artfully producing these titles. Finally, thanks to Mary Vaughn for her steady hand and constant patience.

Elaine Kirn
Santa Monica, CA

Printing 10 9 8 7 6 5 4 3

ISBN 0-13-796798-5

Printed in the United States of America

PART 1

GETTING STARTED

Look at the pictures and talk about them. What do you think is happening? What do you think will happen next?

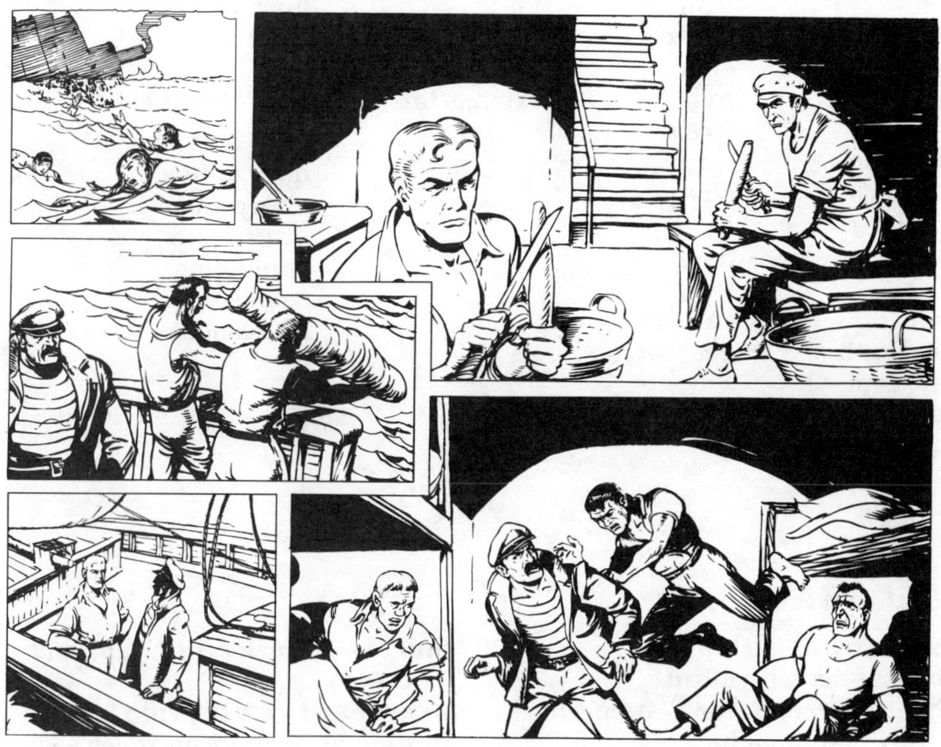

As you read Part 1, think about the answers to these questions.

1 Why was Humphrey Van Weyden aboard the "Ghost"? How did he feel about the situation?
2 How did Van Weyden and the cook get along? What happened between them?
3 How did Captain Larsen and the crew get along? What are some things that they did to each other?
4 What were some of Wolf Larsen's ideas about life?

VOCABULARY

Here are some words you will see in Part 1. Many of them are defined in the Glossary.

nouns	verbs	adjectives	adverbs
crew	lean	cruel	aboard
mate	lower	brutal	overboard
wolf	sink	scornful	
seal	hunt	immortal	**expressions**
skin	treat		earn a living
weapon	warn		obey orders
life belt	sharpen		check a pulse
lifeboat	knife		brute force
wave	dare		card game
fog	tempt		cold-hearted
soul	call off		cold-blooded
strength	get along		
attempt			
panic			
greed			
scorn			
morals			

GLOSSARY

aboard on a ship
brutal cruel, violent
brute force animal strength, with no thought
cold-blooded / **cold-hearted** without feeling, cruel
fog cloudlike moisture in the air which makes it hard to see
greed a desire to have more and more for oneself
immortal never dying
knife *(verb)* stick a knife into someone
morals principals of right and wrong
overboard off the ship
panic strong, uncontrolled fear
scorn low regard for others
sharpen make sharp
sink go down in water
soul the human spirit separate from the body
warn give notice to; tell to be careful
weapon anything used to fight with

JACK LONDON'S SEA WOLF
HUMPHREY VAN WEYDEN
MAUD BREWSTER
GHOST
WOLF LARSEN
Because of many strange and unexpected events, Humphrey Van Weyden and Maud Brewster found themselves aboard the "Ghost." The captain of this ship was the cruel and terrible Wolf Larsen. This is the story of a dangerous and brutal voyage, and of two passengers, who were weak at first, but who found great strength in hard times.

*a boat that carries passengers short distances

Much later, Van Weyden was pulled half dead from the water by the crew of a passing ship.

That's enough, Yonson. Any more and you'll rub the gentleman's skin off.

And how are you feeling now, sir?

Full of water.

What ship is this and where is it going?

This ship is the "Ghost." We're on our way to Japan to hunt seals.

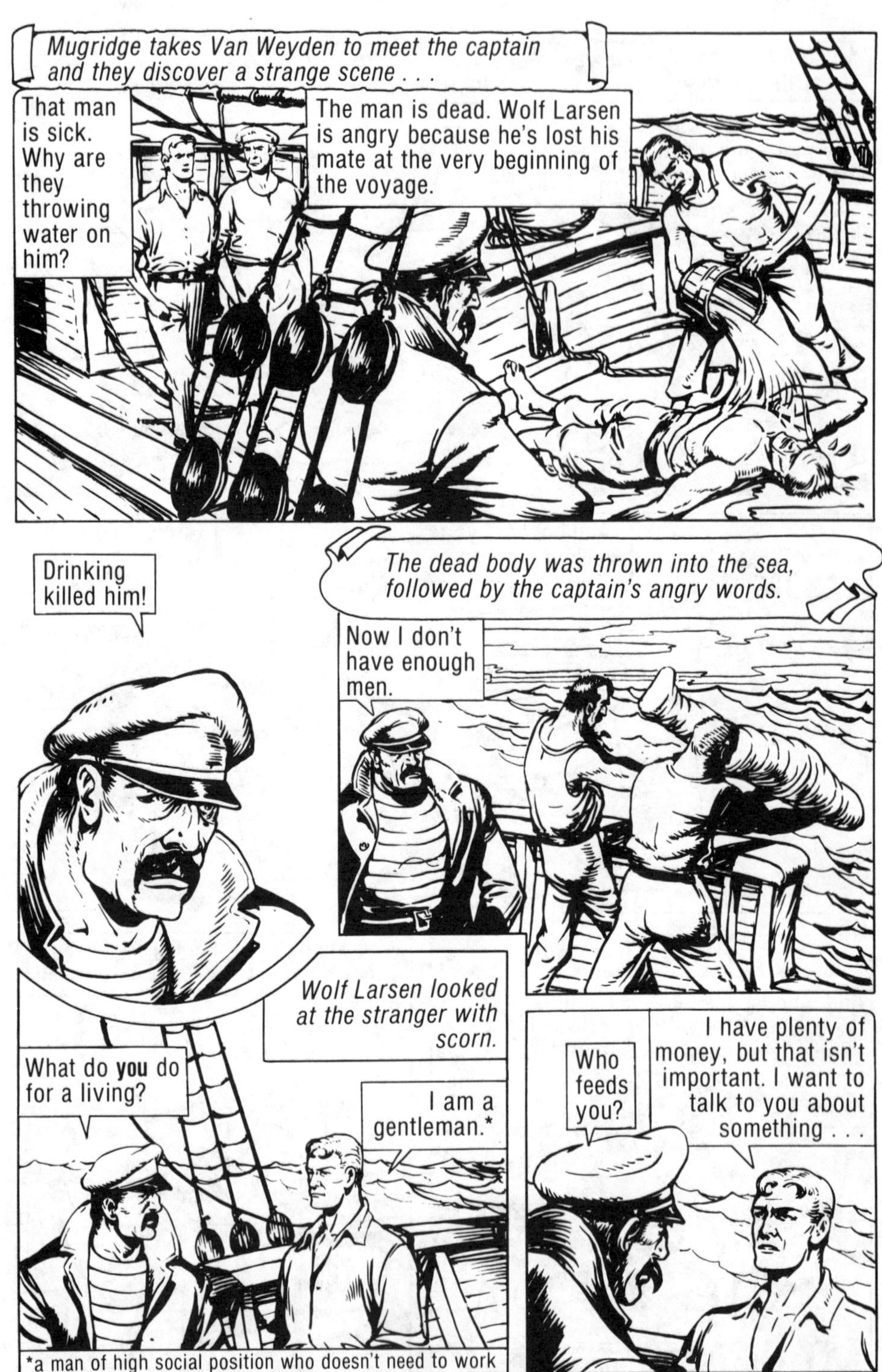
Mugridge takes Van Weyden to meet the captain and they discover a strange scene . . .
That man is sick. Why are they throwing water on him?
The man is dead. Wolf Larsen is angry because he's lost his mate at the very beginning of the voyage.
Drinking killed him!
The dead body was thrown into the sea, followed by the captain's angry words.
Now I don't have enough men.
Wolf Larsen looked at the stranger with scorn.
What do **you** do for a living?
I am a gentleman.*
*a man of high social position who doesn't need to work
Who feeds you?
I have plenty of money, but that isn't important. I want to talk to you about something . . .

Although he didn't like this plan at all, Van Weyden had no choice. He obeyed Wolf Larsen's orders. The cook immediately began to treat him with scorn.

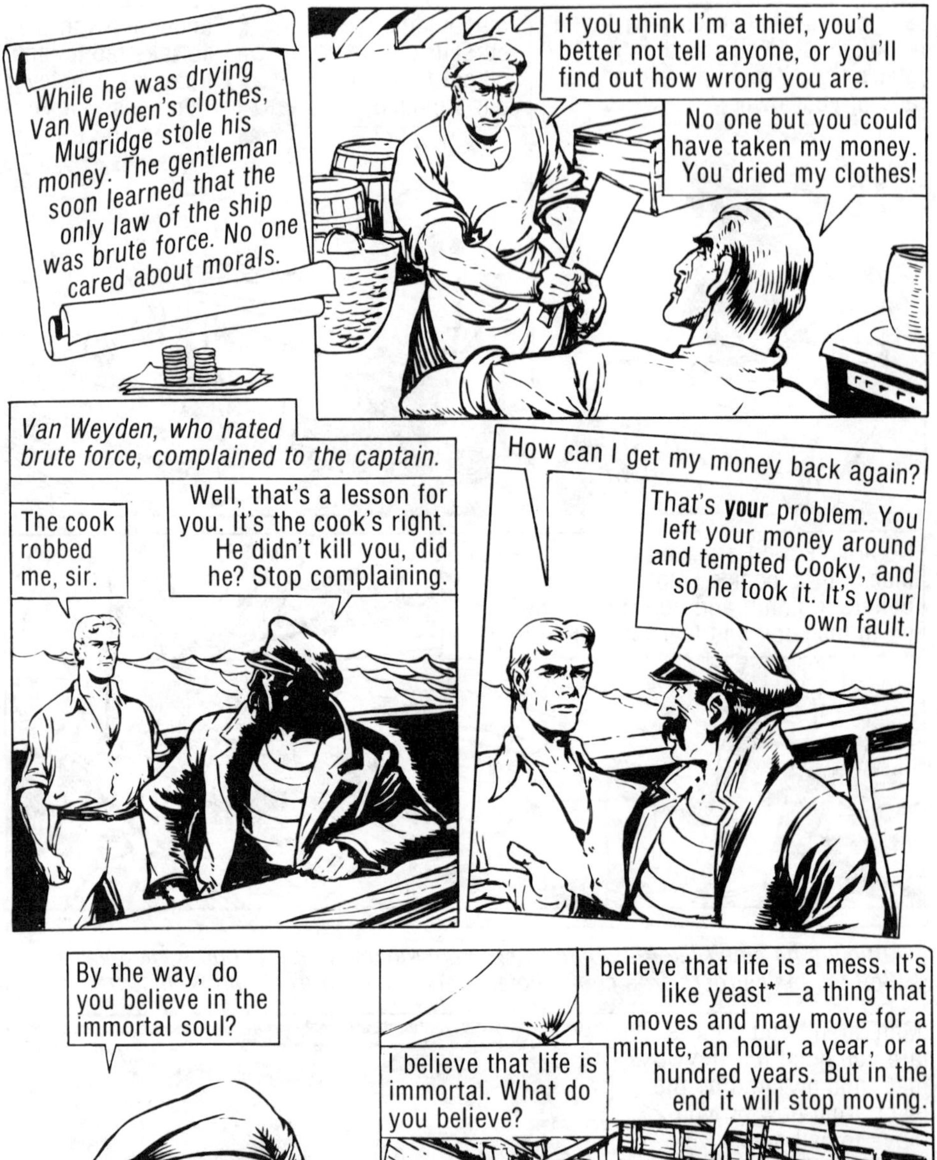

While he was drying Van Weyden's clothes, Mugridge stole his money. The gentleman soon learned that the only law of the ship was brute force. No one cared about morals.

If you think I'm a thief, you'd better not tell anyone, or you'll find out how wrong you are.

No one but you could have taken my money. You dried my clothes!

Van Weyden, who hated brute force, complained to the captain.

The cook robbed me, sir.

Well, that's a lesson for you. It's the cook's right. He didn't kill you, did he? Stop complaining.

How can I get my money back again?

That's **your** problem. You left your money around and tempted Cooky, and so he took it. It's your own fault.

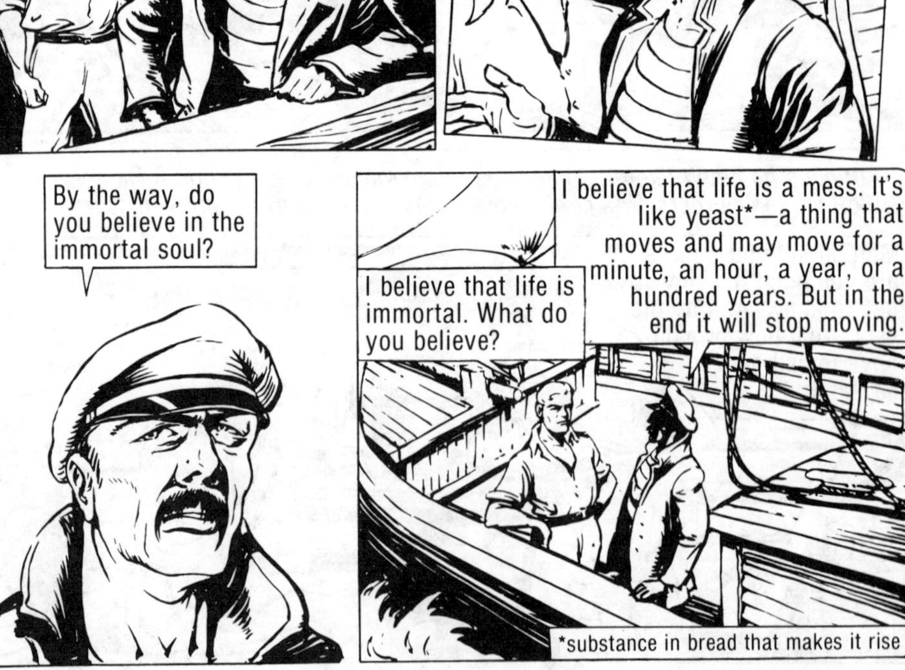

The big eat the little. The strong eat the weak. The lucky eat the most. **You** would like to go back to land, where **your** greed wins.
GHOST
I feel like keeping you here. Here **my** greed will win.
I could kill you now with one hand because you are so weak. But I keep you. Why?
Because you are stronger.
But why am I stronger? Because I have a little more yeast than you? By the way, how much of your money did Cooky steal?
One hundred and eighty-five dollars, sir.
And so Wolf Larsen ended the discussion of the mysteries of life.

As time passed, Van Weyden learned, from a shipmate named Louis, to expect the worst . . .
This is the worst ship on the sea. The mate was the first to die. But there will be more deaths before this voyage is over.
Have you known Captain Larsen very long?

I've known him long and well. Two years ago, he shot four of his men. I was on another ship, not very far away.

Wolf Larsen is his name and he's really a wolf. He's not cold-hearted—he has no heart at all.
How does he get men to work on his ship?

I was drunk when I wrote my name down. But remember—I've never said a word to you about him.
Don't worry. I won't repeat anything you've said.

From 5:30 in the morning till 10:00 at night, Van Weyden, the former gentleman, worked hard for everyone . . .

But one evening, there was a strange card game—strange, because a captain is seldom friendly with a cook.

Bring out the cigars for my "guest," Van Weyden.

I've got money, plenty of it.

The captain's "guest" lost all of his money and was soon very drunk.

The one hundred and eighty-five dollars you won from Mugridge is my money.

It **was** your money, you mean.

For the next three days, however, Van Weyden did nothing but eat at the captain's table and discuss life and literature. He had three peaceful days of rest. But a friendly shipmate warned him . . .

Just when you think he's friendly to you, he hits you like a storm and changes a quiet sea to wild waves.

After that, Van Weyden was again invited to the captain's table. There he complained about the cook.
He says he's going to knife me.
So you're afraid of him.
I'm afraid of that knife, captain.
You said you believe in your immortal soul. Yet you're afraid to die.
Why, my dear man, you'll live forever. Your soul is immortal. So what are you afraid of? Cooky can't hurt you. He can only help you on the way to immortal life.
Or, better still, why don't you help Cooky? Why don't you put a knife into him first? Then I'll give you his job.
He's right. I have to fight Mugridge with his own weapon. I'll get a knife from Louis.
The next morning, Van Weyden and Mugridge looked scornfully at each other as they sharpened their weapons.
I wonder if he can hear my heart beating.

The sailors gave advice to the knife-sharpeners.

Leave his ribs alone, Van Weyden.

Twist your knife into him good, Cooky.

Put it in his stomach, Van.

They're all wolves. Not one would help even if we fought each other to the death.

I thought I'd frighten this "gentleman," but now I'm in trouble.

Not one of those sailors is thinking about my fine cooking. They all want me to die . . . but I won't . . . I'll show them!

The Sea Wolf's brutality increased as the "Ghost" got nearer to the seal-hunting grounds. Mugridge went around listening to the sailors and reported their fights to the captain.
Henderson and Smoke are going to shoot at each other.
Tell them that I'm going to kill the one who wins.
He's as cold-blooded as a fish.
I would let them kill and eat each other, but I need them for seal hunting.
The captain was surprised a while later when a sailor asked for something.
These oilskins are no good. I need better ones, sir.
I'm going to give you something else you don't want.
The captain and his first mate, Johansen, beat the sailor.
That's enough, Johansen. Throw him below.

A few nights later some of the crew turned against cruel Captain Wolf Larsen and beat him . . .
Throw him overboard! Get the mate next!
The sailors did not know the strength of their captain . . .
The man held the ship's line with animal strength and climbed back onto the ship.
Where's the mate?
I don't know, sir. I saw him go forward.*
*to the front of the ship
I went in that direction too, but you see that I didn't come back the same way.

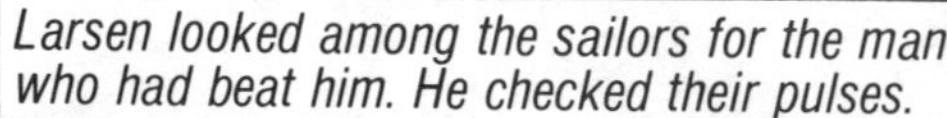
Larsen looked among the sailors for the man who had beat him. He checked their pulses.

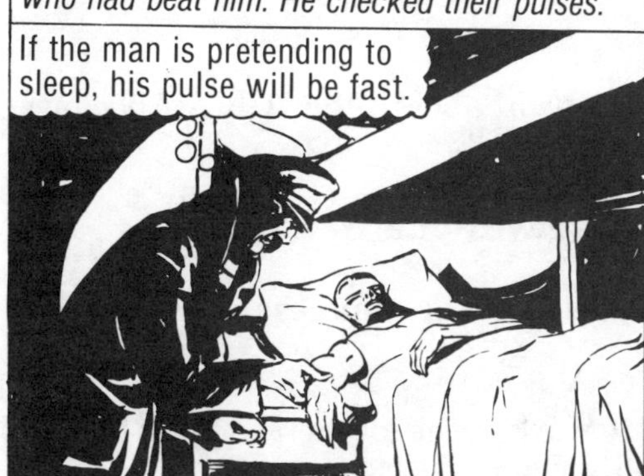
If the man is pretending to sleep, his pulse will be fast.

The man who attacked me has to be here.

Larsen and Johansen had cruelly beaten Johnson a few nights before. Now Johnson watched Larsen carefully from above. Then, as Larsen checked the pulse of the man below, Johnson jumped on him.
Get a knife and we'll finish him as we finished the mate.
I've got him!

During the fight the light was broken, so they fought on in the dark.
Don't let the dog escape!

But the captain did escape in the dark and came back to show he was still in charge.
You animals! You'll pay for this attempt on my life! I'll break every one of you before you leave this ship!

GETTING THE MAIN IDEA

Write TRUE or FALSE.

1 _false_ Humphrey van Weyden went aboard the "Ghost" because he wanted to hunt seals.

2 ________ The crew of the "Ghost" saved Van Weyden's life.

3 ________ Van Weyden was surprised at the kindness of the ship's captain and crew.

4 ________ Van Weyden wanted to work in the kitchen because he had no money to pay for his voyage.

5 ________ The captain ran the ship with brute force; no one worried about morals.

6 ________ The captain believed that life was beautiful and that people were good.

7 ________ Captain Larsen could be friendly one moment and brutal the next moment.

8 ________ The cook planned to kill Van Weyden, but Van Weyden frightened the cook.

9 ________ The captain only cared about the lives of the crew because he needed them to hunt seals.

10 ________ The crew always obeyed Wolf Larsen because they liked his strength.

UNDERSTANDING DETAILS

Circle the letters of ALL the correct answers.

1 Why did Van Weyden find himself aboard the ship "Ghost"?
- (a) The ferryboat he was on sank.
- b He wanted to write about seal hunting.
- (c) The crew of the ship found him in the sea.
- d He was a good cook.

2 What happened between Van Weyden and Mugridge?
- a The gentleman had to work for the cook.
- b Van Weyden won Mugridge's money in a card game.
- c The cook and Van Weyden frightened each other with knives.
- d The two men became good friends.

3 What did Captain Larsen believe about life and men?
- a Men acted from greed.
- b Sailors did not know or care about morals.
- c Life would never end because it was immortal.
- d Men shouldn't have to work for a living.

4 What did Wolf Larsen do to the men of his crew?
- a He ordered the dead mate to be thrown overboard.
- b He forgave the men who tried to kill him.
- c He invited the crew to dinner at his table.
- d He beat a sailor who asked for an oilskin.

5 What did some of the men do to Captain Larsen?
- a They always told him the truth.
- b They beat him and threw him overboard.
- c They said bad things about him behind his back.
- d They gave him money.

Match the descriptions with the names. Write the letters on the lines.

1 __e__ A writer and a gentleman
2 _____ A ferryboat that sank
3 _____ A thief who stole Van Weyden's money
4 _____ A man who talked to Van Weyden of life and literature
5 _____ A shipmate who talked to Van Weyden about Larsen
6 _____ A man who jumped on Larsen as he checked pulses

a Johnson
b Martinez
c Louis
d Larsen
e Van Weyden
f Mugridge

BUILDING VOCABULARY

Write the correct words in the blanks. Choose from these words.

immortal	√fog	shake	force
sharpen	obey	hunt	earn

1 a heavy __fog__ over the bay
2 the __________ soul
3 __________ and kill seals
4 __________ a living
5 __________ orders
6 the law of brute __________
7 __________ a knife
8 __________ hands

Write *p* before the words with positive (good) meanings. Write *n* before the words with negative (bad) meanings.

1 __n__ panic
2 __p__ morals
3 ______ scorn
4 ______ mess
5 ______ fault
6 ______ strength
7 ______ greed
8 ______ complain
9 ______ immortal
10 ______ lucky
11 ______ gentleman
12 ______ peaceful
13 ______ cold-blooded
14 ______ careful
15 ______ greed

Circle the two words in each group that have similar meanings.

1 (crew) gentleman (sailors)

2 frightened afraid former

3 climb rob steal

4 beat hit escape

5 skin heart soul

6 ribs wolf animal

7 knife cigar weapon

8 cruel worried brutal

Turn back to page 1. Answer the questions.

PART 2

GETTING STARTED

Review Part 1 of the story. Tell the important events. Then look at the pictures and talk about them. What do you think is happening? What do you think will happen next?

As you read Part 2, think about the answers to these questions.

1. How did the "Ghost" lose some of its boats and men?
2. Who was the woman aboard the ship and why was she there? How did she feel about her situation?
3. How did Captain Larsen punish the cook? What happened to Mugridge during the punishment?

VOCABULARY

Here are some words you will see in Part 2. Many of them are defined in the Glossary.

nouns	verbs	adjectives	expressions
deserter	desert	furious	lay hands on
deck	disobey	helpless	get back at
prison	punish	unfortunate	be better off
shark	drown		used to
jaw	suffer		be in charge
ankle	disappear		
revenge	row		
shipwreck			
victim			

GLOSSARY

ankle the joint between the foot and leg
deck the floor of a ship
desert to run away from; abandon
deserter a sailor who leaves a ship without permission
disobey not follow orders
drown die under water from lack of oxygen
furious very angry
get back at do something bad to someone in return for his actions
helpless unable to help oneself
lay hands on physically hurt with one's own hands
punish cause pain to someone who did something bad
revenge punishment of someone for having done something bad
shipwreck the destruction of a ship
suffer feel pain

A while later, Van Weyden was called to the captain's cabin.
You'll be the new mate. You'll give orders to the men and they'll have to call you Mr. Van Weyden.
But I know nothing about ships.

But I don't want to be in charge. I have no experience.
That's not necessary at all.

You are now the first mate, Mr.Van Weyden.

Larsen needed all his men, so he didn't put anyone in prison. But he never forgot that they had tried to kill him. Several days later, the "Ghost" met a great herd* of seals.
*a group

The ship followed the seals north. The killing was terrible, and was done only to get fur for coats.

The decks were covered with skins,* dead seals, and blood. The men were busy removing the skins from the dead animals.
*fur of an animal removed from its body

The six boats of the "Ghost" sailed far from the ship, looking for more seals.

One day, when the small boats were all out . . .
Sir, a storm is coming. Shouldn't we call back the boats?
This will be more than just a storm! But we won't call the boats.

Soon a terrible storm hit. After hours of hard search, the ship picked up one of the boats and its crew. Later, they saw another overturned boat, with its crew hanging on. After a lot of hard work, they brought the boat and the men aboard the "Ghost."

Some hours later, they saw another overturned boat, but with no men near it. Against the wishes of the others, Larsen gave orders to save it.

They brought the boat in, but one sailor was killed in the attempt and many others were hurt.

Four days later, the "Ghost" met some sailing ships. The ships were also searching for lost boats. The "Ghost" got back two boats and three crews that had been saved by the other ships. So the total loss was one boat and four men.

The former gentleman millionaire, Van Weyden, was fast becoming a very good seaman.
One day one of the sailors, Leach, came to talk to Van Weyden. Leach hated the captain.
Mr. Van Weyden, how far are we from Japan?
Five hundred miles, west-northwest.
That night, Leach and Johnson deserted the "Ghost" in a seal boat and traveled secretly away towards Japan.
We'll get on another ship in Japan.
If we can escape from Wolf Larsen—I'm sure he'll be looking for us.
Wolf Larsen was furious about the escape of Leach and Johnson. He ordered two men to search the seas for their boat.
I'll get those two dogs if I have to search every mile of the Pacific Ocean!

They searched and searched, and on the third day . . .
There's a boat!

The "Ghost" sailed toward the small boat.

The crew watched as the ship sailed near the boat.
Captain, there are five men in that boat!
That isn't Leach and Johnson!
We lose two men and get five!
Larsen will like that!
They'll live to wish we hadn't seen them!

Look! I think there's a woman in the boat!

When the strangers were on board . . .
Mr. Van Weyden, take the lady below and see that she is comfortable.
Thank you, sir. My name is Maud Brewster.
The shipwrecked men were taken into the crew right away.
When will we get to Japan?
Ha! I can see that you don't know Wolf Larsen!
You gentlemen are our new shipmates.
We were expecting to see land this morning. Shouldn't we be in Japan soon?
Our captain is a strange man. You'll have to be prepared for anything.
But I thought it was the custom of the sea to help all victims of shipwrecks.
I only want to prepare you for the worst—if the worst happens.
Too bad we saw those shipwrecked people. They'd be better off if they had reached land in their boat.
They wouldn't have made it in the boat, sir. Another storm is coming.

It was lucky that we found those shipwrecked people. We'll make sailors out of them—or at least they can row the boats.
What about Miss Brewster?

I don't know what to do with her—yet!

Are you going to continue to search for Leach and Johnson?
I don't know. You see, with these new men, I have all the crew I need.

And I'm sure Leach and Johnson have been having a hard time. Why don't you forgive them? If they deserted, they were forced into it.
By me?

By you! I'm warning you, Wolf Larsen. If you hurt those poor men, I'll kill you!

The captain surprised everyone with his answer.
If I promise not to lay my hands on Leach and Johnson, will you promise not to try to kill me?
I promise!

Later, Maud Brewster came to talk to Wolf Larsen.
When will we arrive in Japan?
In four months, maybe three, when we finish hunting seals.
I . . . I thought . . . They told me that we could reach Japan in a day. It . . . It isn't right.
It may be **your** bad luck that you have to stay with us, but it's **our** good luck.
What do you think, Mr. Van Weyden?
If, as you say, you were going to Japan for your health . . .
I can promise you that your health will get much better here aboard the "Ghost"!
We're very friendly on the "Ghost." Mr. Van Weyden has learned that. We'll do anything to make our guests feel comfortable.
Even let us peel* potatoes and wash dishes.
*take the skins off of

Hours later, the "Ghost" saw Leach and Johnson in their boat. They were in trouble.

Those men will never make it to* land in that boat. They'll die unless Wolf Larsen helps them. Their boat is sinking.

*reach

I may be picked up by some passing ship.
There will be no passing ship.
I have no clothes—nothing, sir. You have to understand that I am not used to such a life.
You'll get used to it soon. The sooner, the better.
I'll give you cloth, needles, and thread.* I hope it won't be too hard for you to make yourself a dress.
*things to sew with
Wolf Larsen seemed angry that his woman passenger kept calm.
What right do you have to live when you do no work? Have you ever earned a dollar?
Right now I earn about eighteen hundred dollars a year!
Larsen and Van Weyden learned that their passenger was a writer.
Well, all right. We'll feed you during the time you're aboard the ship.

Wolf Larsen had warned the cook about his dirty kitchen. He said he would punish him if he didn't change.
I warned you, Cooky, and now it's time for your punishment.

Mugridge was afraid and tried to get away.

He climbed up the ropes, but Larsen ordered the men to bring him down.

Finally, they caught the unlucky cook and brought him down to the deck.

Please, sir
—oh, Captain!
Please don't
throw me
overboard!
I'll never
disobey you
again, sir!
Please,
Captain!
Cooky, I warned
you, and now
you must be
punished!
They tied a rope around the poor Mugridge
and thew him overboard.
Cooky's going
to get a bath!
Oh, the
poor fish!
GHOST
Yeowww!
Aboard the ship, the men were laughing at
their poor shipmate. In the cold water, the
frightened cook looked around for sharks.
The crew didn't hear his shouts for help.
Are you trying
to catch fish
with that rope?
Aye, miss. We
just caught
the cook!
Ha, ha,
ha, ha!

The ship went up and down, pulling Mugridge in and out of the water. Though he didn't drown, he suffered the pain of half-drowning.
GHOST
Suddenly, aboard the ship, one of the crew saw danger.
There's a shark!
Pull Cooky in! Fast!
Pull me in! Hurry, hurry, hurry!
Pull!
Fast!
Hurry, men, or he'll be finished!
Ho!

They pulled the cook out of the water, but the shark jumped after him.
Yeowww!
GHOST
The cook was pulled in like a fish. His right foot was gone, cut off at the ankle.
The shark got him!
His foot's gone!
Tie his leg! Stop the blood!
Wolf Larsen, you did this to me!
Half-crazy with pain, Mugridge sank his teeth into Larsen's leg, but Larsen shook himself free.
That's enough, man! The punishment didn't call for a shark.
We didn't plan on the shark. This was a game of men, maybe harder than you are used to, but still just a game of men. The shark wasn't part of the game. It was just bad luck.

Wolf Larsen planned his revenge on the shark. The men caught the animal and pulled him aboard.
Now we'll get back at the shark for taking the cook's foot.
They pulled the shark up and opened his jaws.
Open the jaws. And we'll give him something to close them on.
A stake,* sharpened at both ends, was put in the shark's mouth so that he couldn't close his jaws.
Now throw him overboard.
He'll never bite another sailor.
He'll never bite anything at all.
*a strong stick
GHOST
The shark was returned to the sea, helpless, to die from hunger.

GETTING THE MAIN IDEA

Complete the sentences. Circle the correct answers.

1 Captain Larsen made Van Weyden (a seal hunter/the new mate) even though Van Weyden didn't want to (give orders/sail the ship).

2 The captain sent the sailors out in boats to (hunt seals/rob ships); some men (drowned/ran away) because he didn't (find any seals/call back the boats) before a storm.

3 Two sailors (escaped from/destroyed) the "Ghost"; Wolf Larsen wanted to find and (punish/free) them.

4 The "Ghost" (picked up/hit) five people in a boat, including one (captain/woman); Larsen forced the men to (sail back to land/work for him).

5 Larsen promised not to (lay hands on/search for) Leach and Johnson himself, so he let them (desert the ship/drown).

6 The captain punished the cook by (not feeding him/pulling him on a rope in the water); when the men pulled the cook back into the ship, he (lost his foot to/had caught) a shark.

UNDERSTANDING DETAILS

Write the correct names in the blanks. Choose from these names.

Wolf Larsen	Maud Brewster	Kerfoot and Mugridge
Van Weyden	the cook	Leach and Johnson

1 Wolf Larsen said to Van Weyden, "You are now the first mate."

2 ________________ said about ________________, "We'll cut off the finger . . . and wait until morning . . . to set his ribs."

3 ________________ said about ________________, "I'll get those two dogs if I have to search every mile . . . ."

4 ________________ said to ________________, "I only want to prepare you for the worst."

5 ________________ said to ________________, "I have no clothes . . . I'm not used to such a life."

6 ________________ said to ________________, "Please don't throw me overboard. I'll never disobey you again."

7 ________________ said to ________________, "The shark wasn't part of the game. It was just bad luck."

Match the parts of the sentences. Write the letters on the lines.

1 The ship followed the seals e

2 Larsen gave orders that risked men's lives ________

3 Leach and Johnson deserted the "Ghost" ________

4 Larsen kept the shipwrecked people on the ship ________

5 Larsen promised not to lay hands on Leach and Johnson ________

6 Larsen ordered the men to throw the cook overboard ______

7 The crew pulled Mugridge from the sea ________

8 The crew put a stake in the shark's jaws ________

a to save him from a shark.

b to punish him for having a dirty kitchen.

c to get away from Wolf Larsen.

d to punish him for taking the cook's foot.

e to kill them for skins.

f to get more sailors for his crew.

g to save a small boat.

h to get a promise that Van Weyden wouldn't kill him.

BUILDING VOCABULARY

Which word doesn't belong in each group? Cross it out.

1 stranger
gentleman
~~danger~~
deserter

2 seal
wolf
shark
passenger

3 health
jaw
ribs
ankle

4 lifeboat
wave
cabin
deck

5 writer
mate
captain
sailor

6 force
order
continue
punish

7 complain
promise
refuse
climb

8 lucky
broken
lost
hurt

9 furious
angry
calm
crazy

Write the correct words in the blanks. Choose from these words.

prepare	shipwreck	cover	suffer	bite
remove	pretend	drown	✓check	overturn

1 Larsen ___check___ed the pulses of the men to see if they were just ____________ing to sleep.

2 The crew hung on to the ____________ed boat because they didn't want to ____________.

3 Blood ____________ed the deck of the ship when the men ____________ed the skins of the seals.

4 Some of the people were sailing in a life boat because they had been ____________ed.

5 Van Weyden told Maud Brewster terrible things about the captain to ____________ her for the worst.

6 Cooky ____________ed a lot of pain as the ship pulled him through the cold water.

7 The men returned the shark to the sea with a stake in its mouth so it couldn't ____________ anything.

PART 3

GETTING STARTED

Review Parts 1 and 2 of the story. Tell the important events. Then look at the pictures and talk about them. What do you think is happening? What do you think will happen next?

As you read Part 3, think about the answers to these questions.

1 What happened when the "Ghost" met the "Macedonia"?
2 How did Van Weyden and Brewster escape?
3 What did Larsen try to do when the ship was on the beach?
4 What happened to Larsen, Van Weyden, and Brewster in the end?

VOCABULARY

Here are some words you will see in Part 3. Most of them are defined in the Glossary.

nouns	verbs	adjectives	expressions
prisoner	land	drunken	pay attention to
monster	fool	frozen	set fire to
hut	wreck	paralyzed	
handcuffs	bury		
attempt	risk		
	pretend		

GLOSSARY

bury put under the ground
drunken under the influence of alcohol
fool pay a trick on; deceive
frozen as cold as ice; solid
handcuffs two connected bracelets that keep the hands together so that a person can't use them
hut a small house
land go onto land from the sea
paralyzed completely unable to move
wreck damage greatly; destroy

Sometime later . . .
Is it true that Captain Larsen let two of his men drown?
It's true.

And you did nothing to stop him?
I couldn't stop him.

Maud seemed disappointed by Van Weyden's answer.
What's your advice? That I kill this man Larsen? Or that I kill myself?
No, not that! But what can be done?

You have to understand that this man Larsen is a monster! Don't make him angry. Be friendly with him. Discuss life and literature with him. You'll find that he's an interested listener and is intelligent. And try not to pay attention to the cruelty on the ship. We don't have the strength to fight the man with force. We'll have to win with our brains. Do as I say and you'll soon find that I'm right.

The "Ghost" continued to follow the seals.
One day, the "Ghost" met the "Macedonia." The captain of this ship was Death Larsen, Wolf Larsen's brother!
There's the "Macedonia"!
That's my brother's ship. He'll try to keep us from the seals!
You see, Van Weyden . . . they're taking our seals! They're shooting at our crew!
What are you going to do?
Do? I'm going to give the men guns, of course! We'll fight them for the seals!
GHOST

Just then, a shot hit the ship just above their heads.
Maud, maybe you'd better go below.
No, I'll stay here.
I like you a lot better for your decision. You could be the wife of a pirate* captain.
*sea robber
The "Ghost" caught one of the "Macedonia's" boats.
Take those men aboard and lock them up.
Then Larsen began shooting at the other boats of the "Macedonia." And he usually hit them.
One man is dead. I wish I had hit Death Larsen.
He'd shoot his own brother!
Larsen's brute force won over the boat rowers of the "Macedonia" and Death Larsen's sailors became prisoners.
The "Macedonia" is coming after us, sir, and it has guns aboard.
We'll lose her in the fog ahead. From then on, it will be clear sailing.
Sailors from both ships became friends as Wolf Larsen passed drinks among them to celebrate his victory over his brother.

While his men were getting drunk, Wolf Larsen drank nothing. He couldn't risk it.
Late that night, Wolf Larsen turned the wheel over to Van Weyden and went to sleep. With the drunken crew sleeping deeply, Van Weyden and Maud Brewster were the only two on deck. It was then that they tried to escape from the "Ghost."
Will you trust yourself to me for a voyage of six hundred miles or so?
You mean in an open boat? Yes!
They filled the boat with food, water, warm clothing, skins, guns, and knives and then set out on the sea . . .
We're six hundred miles from Japan. If the wind continues, we'll make it in five days.
And if there's a storm, can this little boat take it?
It would have to be a very big storm to wreck this strong boat!

Can you swim?

No.

Neither can I. We have to get to land without swimming. We'll look for some opening between the rocks.

I think it's a rookery.*

*a place where seals live

With some good luck, they found a beach to land on and tied up the boat.

I think we need a hot cup of coffee first.

Anything hot —I'm frozen inside and out.

They found the island deserted and knew they would have to spend the winter there. Van Weyden and Maud began to build two huts, and they covered them with seal skins. They used the oil from the seals' fat for light and heat.

When he got up one morning, Van Weyden was surprised to see the "Ghost" on the beach.
If Larsen is aboard, I could kill him in his sleep.
Carrying a knife and a gun, Van Weyden searched the ship.
It's deserted. There's no one aboard.
But coming around a corner, Van Weyden suddenly met Wolf Larsen.
Well, why don't you shoot?
Van Weyden was silent with fear.
You can't do it. You wouldn't kill a man with no weapons.
I know it.
There are seals here. They woke me up with their noise. I've been hunting for a rookery for years.

Where is the crew? Why are you on the ship all alone?
My brother caught me and stole all my men. I was left alone on my own ship.

But how did you lose the sails?
Look at them.

They were cut with a knife!
Not completely. It was more clever. Look again.

Van Weyden looked closely and saw that the lines had been almost cut through. Just enough was left to hold the sails for a short time. But when a heavy wind came up, the ropes broke.
Cooky did that. He wanted to get back at me for feeding him to the shark.

I guess you've got me where you want me now,Van Weyden.
No, I haven't. I want you thousands of miles from here.

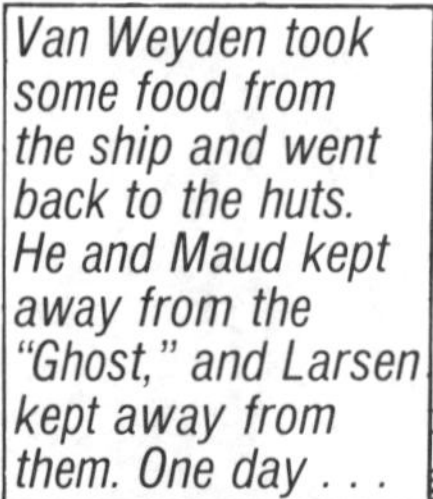

If the floor doesn't make any noise, he'll never hear me. Let him think I'm below.

Van Weyden went back to Maud and told her what had happened.
It's too bad the "Ghost" has lost her sails. We could sail away in her.
Hmmm . . . that's a good idea! Maybe . . .
That afternoon, Van Weyden went back to the ship with Maud and spoke to Larsen, who was surprised that he was not a prisoner . . .
It's you, is it? So you fooled me this morning. What do you want?
I want to put the sails back on the ship and sail away!
I order you not to touch my ship!
You have never thought about morals before. You don't think I'm going to think about them now with you, do you?
I tell you again . . . you'd better leave things alone.
Don't you want to escape with us?
No. I plan to die here.
Well, we don't!

Not listening to Larsen, Maud and Van Weyden, with hard work, raised the first sail.
Larsen says he's going to sink the ship, or set fire to it.
If we're going to escape from this island, we'll have to make him a prisoner.
Larsen made plans to get Van Weyden. One day, he pretended he was sick.
I have to be careful. He may be pretending.
I'll kill him when he comes near.
Maud screamed as she saw Wolf Larsen catch Van Weyden around the neck.
Van Weyden fought to shake himself loose and Larsen had to let go. Van Weyden got away from him fast.
You must never trust him again.
Now that we have him helpless, he'll stay helpless. There are handcuffs in his cabin.

Larsen had a stroke* and was almost completely paralyzed.
It's possible that you'll get better, Larsen.
There's no longer any need for handcuffs. I'm a paralytic** now.
*a sudden loss of blood from the brain
**person who is paralyzed
Van Weyden and Maud worked hard to repair the ship once again.
When we get back home, we can write about the sea.
If our plan works!

The wolf was paralyzed, but not too helpless to try to destroy the ship. One afternoon . . .
Fire!
The wolf is not yet completely dead!

Larsen had set fire to his bed in an attempt to burn the ship.
No, you won't, Larsen!
I'll destroy both of you yet!

After more days of hard work, the "Ghost" was ready to sail into deep water once again.
When I raise the anchor,* you'll have to take the wheel.
I'll have to raise the sail at the same time.
*a heavy weight that keeps the ship from moving

The two shipwrecked people, the gentleman and the lady, had become very good sailors . . .
The wind is strong. And now, if you can raise the right sail, we might be on our way.
I'll do my best.

The winds were good to Maud and Van Weyden.
The old ship is moving again . . .
GHOST

We made it! We're on our way!
I have to go and see our prisoner!

But when Maud got to Larsen . . .
He's dead!
Wolf Larsen was buried that day.
I have the feeling that he will never really leave the "Ghost."
His spirit will sail the seas forever.
As they spoke, a small ship appeared a few miles away.
Look . . . there's a ship!
And it's coming our way! We're saved!
It's painted black . . .
That means it's a United States ship.
Before long, they were aboard the American ship, looking back toward their island . . .
Goodbye, island.
And goodbye to you, Wolf Larsen.
The End

GETTING THE MAIN IDEA

Write TRUE or FALSE before the *parts* of the sentences.

1 __true__ Wolf Larsen wanted to fight against his brother
__false__ because Death Larsen was a kind sea captain.

2 ________ Van Weyden and Maud were afraid to escape from the ship
________ because they weren't sailors and couldn't swim.

3 ________ Wolf Larsen came to the deserted island in the "Ghost"
________ because he had promised to pay back the deserters.

4 ________ Van Weyden never went aboard the ship on the beach
________ because he didn't want Larsen to take him away from the island.

5 ________ Wolf Larsen tried to make Van Weyden prisoner or kill him
________ because he wanted to win even though he was going to die.

6 ________ Van Weyden and Maud Brewster showed great strength
________ because they killed Wolf Larsen and then killed themselves.

UNDERSTANDING DETAILS

Complete the sentences. Cross out the letter of the ONE *incorrect* answer for each sentence.

1 Van Weyden and Maud Brewster didn't fight Wolf Larsen because they _____
- a weren't strong enough to use force.
- b hadn't planned what to do yet.
- c wanted to use their brains against him.
- d preferred to discuss literature with him.

2 When Wolf Larsen met his brother's ship, he _____
- a fought him for the seals.
- b let Maud go to Japan with Death Larsen.
- c took prisoners from his brother's crew.
- d wanted to shoot his brother.

3 Van Weyden and Maud Brewster were able to escape from the "Ghost" when _____
- a the men were drunk from a victory celebration.
- b they used weapons against the crew.
- c they filled a strong boat with food and other things.
- d they got to land without swimming.

4 When Van Weyden found the "Ghost" on the beach, he learned that _____
- a Larsen wanted help and forgiveness.
- b he couldn't shoot the helpless captain.
- c the cook had caused the captain to lose his sails.
- d Larsen had lost his crew to his brother.

5 Even though the "Sea Wolf"—Wolf Larsen—was blind and sick, he tried to _____
- a keep Van Weyden a prisoner below the trap door.
- b escape from the island.
- c set fire to the ship.
- d kill Van Weyden with his own hands.

6 At the end of the story, Van Weyden and Maud Brewster _____
- a sail on the "Ghost."
- b were saved by a United States ship.
- c buried the Sea Wolf.
- d stayed on the island and fell in love.

BUILDING VOCABULARY

Which three words fit in each blank? Choose from these words.

knives	literature	strangers
passengers	crew	the soul
immortality	force	weapons

1 Van Weyden sometimes discussed literature with Larsen.
immortality
the soul

2 The people aboard the "Ghost" were ______.
______
______

3 The sailors used ______ to hurt each other.
______
______

Choose from these words.

careful	paralyzed	brutal
friendly	blind	calm
helpless	cruel	scornful

1 When he was with Wolf Larsen, Van Weyden tried to be ______.
______
______

2 The Sea Wolf was ______ in his treatment of people.
______
______

3 Just before Wolf Larsen's death, he became ______.
______
______

Choose from these words.

leave	escape	beat
hurt	desert	sink
overturn	wreck	frighten

1 The violent sailors sometimes tried to ____________ each other.
____
____

2 Because they hated life on the ship, some sailors tried to ____________.
____
____

3 A bad storm could ____________ a boat.
____
____

SUMMARIZING

Put the events of the story in correct order. Write the numbers on the lines.

1 ______ Van Weyden and the cook tried to frighten each other with knives.

2 ______ The Sea Wolf died on the ship and Van Weyden and Maud Brewster were saved.

3 ______ The captain forced Van Weyden to work as the cook's helper.

4 ___1___ Because of a shipwreck, a gentleman millionaire found himself aboard the "Ghost."

5 ______ Larsen punished Cooky for disobedience and a shark bit off his foot.

5 ______ The crew threw the captain overboard; he never forgot the attempt on his life.

7 ______ In the search for two deserters, the "Ghost" picked up a shipwrecked woman.

8 ______ Van Weyden and Maud Brewster escaped in a boat to a deserted island.

Discuss the answers to the questions. Tell your opinions.

1 Tell about Wolf Larsen, Van Weyden, and Maud Brewster. What kind of people were they?
2 Why was the Sea Wolf so cruel? Why was there no morality aboard the ship?

Artwork originally appeared elsewhere or in Classics Illustrated No. 85